1

C000182416

With Scriptural Reflections
and Prayers

Edited by
Rev. Victor Hoagland, C.P.

Illustrated by
William Luberoff

Catholic
Classics

Regina Press
New York

Nihil Obstat: Reverend Robert O. Morrisey, J.C.D.
                  Censor librorum
                  January 13th, 2003

Imprimatur: Most Reverend William Murphy
                  Bishop of Rockville Centre
                  January 15th, 2003

THE REGINA PRESS
10 Hub Drive
Melville, New York 11747

ISBN# 0-88271-307-8

Printed in Hong Kong.

The Rosary of the Blessed Virgin Mary

"To recite the rosary is nothing other than to contemplate the face of Christ with Mary."
Pope John Paul II

In his letter "Rosarium Virginis Mariae" October 16, 2002, Pope John Paul II expressed his esteem for a method of praying that has nourished the faith of generations of Christians. The pope called on Catholics – and other Christians as well – to pray the rosary and enter "the school of Mary," who knew Jesus Christ so well as his mother and who was his closest disciple.

Though it is not mandatory, the pope also suggested that five mysteries be added to the traditional fifteen. He called them "Luminous Mysteries," or the Mysteries of Light, which include the mysteries of Christ's public ministry between his Baptism and his Passion. While leaving the use of these mysteries "to the freedom of individuals and communities," Pope John Paul suggested that they could help make the prayer more deeply centered in the life of Christ.

This book includes the Luminous Mysteries, taken from a period of Jesus' life when he revealed himself as "the light of the world," and incorporates them into the fifteen traditional mysteries.

The Rosary and the Scriptures

Pope John Paul II also recommended the use of scriptural verses to accompany each mystery of the rosary in order to deepen the scriptural dimension of this prayer. This book offers short scriptural verses as well as meditations to highlight each mysteries.

The Rosary: Where Did It Come From?

Praying the rosary well is more important than knowing its history, yet knowing the origins of the prayer can teach us much about it.

The beginnings of the rosary are found in the early Christian practice of reciting the 150 psalms from the bible, either daily or weekly, as a way of prayer. Those unable to recite the psalms began to recite 150 payers, mainly the Our Father, 150 times, often using beads to count the prayers. By medieval times the custom of saying "Paternoster" beads (the Latin for Our Father) was common in many countries of

Europe. While saying the prayers it was customary to meditate on the mysteries of the life of Jesus, from his birth to his resurrection.

The rosary in its present form arose in late medieval Christianity when Mary, the Mother of Jesus, was seen as a guide to the mysteries of her Son. A decade of prayers called the Hail Mary was preceded by the Our Father. Meditation on the mysteries of Christ remained at the heart of the prayer.

Through the centuries, saints like St. Dominic, many of the popes, as well as countless ordinary Christians have found the rosary to be a school of prayer and a source of spiritual blessing. It is both simple and profound. Not beyond anyone's reach, its repeated words bring peace to the soul. And the mysteries of Jesus that it recalls are also meant to be repeated on our own. We ask to "imitate what they contain and obtain what they promise, through Christ our Lord."

The Hail Mary

The Hail Mary evolved as a prayer from the devotion of medieval men and women who saw Mary, the mother to Jesus, as the great witness to His life, death and resurrection. Its earliest form was the greeting made to Mary by the Angel Gabriel:

Hail Mary, full of grace, the Lord is with you
LUKE 1:28

Over time the greeting given to Mary by her cousin Elizabeth was added:

Blessed are you among women
and blessed is the fruit of your womb.
LUKE 1:42

Finally by the 15th century, the remainder of the prayer appeared:

Holy Mary, mother of God, pray for us sinners
now and at the hour of our death.

The prayer calls upon Mary, full of grace and close to her Son, to intercede for us sinners now and at the time our death. We share her as a mother with St. John to whom Jesus entrusted her, when on Calvary He said, "Behold your mother." She will always bring Christ into our life. We trust her to care for us as she cared for the newly married couple at Cana in Galilee. We can go to her in our need.

By the end of the 16th century the practice of saying 150 Hail Marys in series or decades of 10 was popular among many ordinary Christian people. The mysteries of the life, death and resurrection of Jesus, contained in the Joyful, Sorrowful and Glorious Mysteries, were remembered during these prayers.

Why We Pray the Rosary

The rosary is a special way of praying. As we recite the prayers of the rosary, we think about certain stories in the lives of Jesus and Mary. These stories are called "mysteries". We use rosary beads to help us keep count of the prayers and the mysteries.

How to Pray the Rosary

The complete rosary consists of twenty decades, but it is further divided into four distinct parts, the Joyful, the Luminous, the Sorrowful, and the Glorious Mysteries, each containing five decades.

To say the rosary, begin by making the sign of the cross and saying the Apostles' Creed on the crucifix, one Our Father on the first bead, three Hail Marys on the next three beads, and then a Glory Be to the Father. When this is finished, meditate upon the first mystery, say an Our Father, ten Hail Marys, and one Glory Be to the Father. The first decade is now completed, and to finish the rosary proceed in the same manner until all five decades have been said. When this is done, say one Hail Holy Queen.

As a prayer of faith, the rosary usually begins with two basic summaries of faith: the Sign of the Cross and the Creed. These prayers invite us to believe in God, the Father, the Son, and Holy Spirit, and to remember God's plan of salvation proclaimed in the scriptures.

The rosary is made up of decades of prayers. A decade of the rosary consists of an Our Father prayed before ten Hail Marys. At the end of a decade the prayer "Glory be to the Father, and to the Son, and to the Holy Spirit"is said. Most rosaries have five decades of beads.

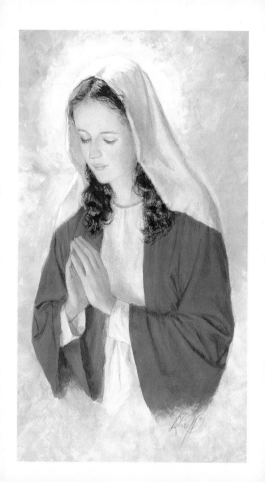

PRAYERS OF THE ROSARY
The Sign of the Cross

In the name of the Father, ✝ and of the Son, and of the Holy Spirit. Amen.

The Apostles' Creed

I believe in God, the Father Almighty, Creator of heaven and earth; and in Jesus Christ, His only Son, our Lord, who was conceived by the Holy Spirit; born of the Virgin Mary, suffered under Pontius Pilate, was crucified, died and was buried. He descended into hell; the third day He rose again from the dead; He ascended into heaven, sitteth at the right hand God the Father Almighty; from thence He shall come to judge the living and the dead. I believe in the Holy Spirit, the Holy Catholic Church, the communion of Saints, the forgiveness of sins, the resurrection of the body, and life everlasting. Amen.

The Our Father

Our Father who art in heaven, hallowed be Thy name; Thy kingdom come; Thy will be done on earth as it is in heaven. Give us this day our daily bread; and forgive us our trespasses as we forgive those who trespass against us. And lead us not into temptation; but deliver us from evil. Amen.

The Hail Mary

Hail Mary, full of grace, the Lord is with you; Blessed are you among women, and blessed is the fruit of your womb, Jesus. Holy Mary, Mother of God, pray for us sinners, now and at the hour our death. Amen.

Glory Be to the Father

Glory be to the Father, and to the Son, and to the Holy Spirit; as it was in the beginning, is now, and ever shall be, world without end. Amen.

The Hail, Holy Queen

Hail, holy Queen, Mother of Mercy! Our life, our sweetness, and our hope! To thee do we cry, poor banished children of Eve; to thee do we send up our sighs, mourning and weeping in this valley of tears. Turn, then, most gracious advocate, thine eyes of mercy toward us; and after this our exile show unto us the blessed fruit of thy womb Jesus; O clement, O loving, O sweet Virgin Mary.

V. Pray for us, O holy Mother of God.

R. That we may be made worthy of the promises of Christ.

The Five Joyful Mysteries

Mondays and Saturdays
FIRST JOYFUL MYSTERY
The Annunciation
The Angel Gabriel tells Mary that
she is to be the Mother of God.

SECOND JOYFUL MYSTERY
The Visitation
The Blessed Virgin pays a visit to
her cousin Elizabeth.

THIRD JOYFUL MYSTERY
The Birth of Jesus
The Infant Jesus is born in a stable
at Bethlehem.

FOURTH JOYFUL MYSTERY
Presentation of Jesus in the Temple
The Blessed Virgin presents the Child
Jesus to Simeon in the Temple.

FIFTH JOYFUL MYSTERY
Finding the Child Jesus in the Temple
Jesus is lost for three days, and the
Blessed Mother finds Him in the Temple.

The Joyful Mysteries

Mondays and Saturdays

1st Joyful Mystery
The Annunciation

The Angel Gabriel appears to Mary, announcing she is to be the Mother of God.

5th Joyful Mystery
The Finding in the Temple

The Blessed Mother finds Jesus in the Temple.

2nd Joyful Mystery
The Visitation

Elizabeth greets Mary: "Blessed art Thou among women and blessed is the fruit of Thy womb!"

4th Joyful Mystery
The Presentation

The Blessed Mother presents the Child Jesus in the Temple.

3rd Joyful Mystery
The Nativity

The Virgin Mary gives birth to the Redeemer of the World.

FIRST JOYFUL MYSTERY

The Annunciation

The Angel Gabriel said: "Do not be afraid, Mary, you have found favor with God. You will conceive and bear a Son, and you shall call him Jesus."   LUKE 1, 30-31

Meditation

Nor was Mary afraid to do God's will. The angel left her, but she was not afraid, even as she faced Joseph's initial doubt, even though she did not fully understand it all. She trusted even through the birth in a poor stable, through the silent years at Nazareth, the mysterious years of Jesus' ministry and the darkest hours of His passion and death.

Mary believed God's purpose for her, even though she did not always understand.

Shall we not say too: "We are your servants, O Lord?" Shall we not say with Mary, "Be it done to me according to your word?"

One Our Father, ten Hail Marys and one Glory Be to the Father.

SECOND JOYFUL MYSTERY

The Visitation

Mary visited her cousin, Elizabeth, who said to her, "Blessed are you among women and blessed is the fruit of your womb."

LUKE 1, 42

Meditation

Such a simple thing: two cousins visit! One blesses the other. Mary, with the mighty Child within her, makes Elizabeth's unborn infant leap for joy. And the elder Elizabeth speaks words of praise to the younger Mary. "Blessed are you..."

A simple visit between two people, yet blessings are exchanged and the two strengthened by God's grace.

Help us, O Lord, to make all our meetings with others, the simple times we share with one another, moments of joy, faith, love and blessings.

One Our Father, ten Hail Marys and one Glory Be to the Father.

THIRD JOYFUL MYSTERY

The Birth of Jesus

"Mary gave birth to her first-born son and wrapped him in swaddling clothes and laid him in a manger." LUKE 2, 7

Meditation

A Child is born for us! In the poorest of places, a stable. With nothing of his own, Jesus Christ was born. He would always be poor, as one of us, and the poor always found a welcome near Him. The shepherds came at the angel's call, leading their sheep. And they returned singing for joy. Later, the blind, the lame and the deaf came. Jesus welcomed them, too. Those possessed by demons, those haunted by fears came; their spirits were lifted and they felt their hearts soar.

Shall we not come too?

"O dying souls, behold your living spring; O dazzled eyes, behold your sun of grace; Dull ears, attend what word this Word doth bring..."

One Our Father, ten Hail Marys and one Glory Be to the Father.

FOURTH JOYFUL MYSTERY

Presentation of Jesus in the Temple

"When the time came...they brought the child up to Jerusalem to present him to the Lord."   LUKE 1, 22

Meditation

For Mary and Joseph the time came, shortly after Jesus' birth, to present Him in the temple to God. The time came too for the old man Simeon and the old woman Anna, waiting and praying so long. Waiting in the temple many years, they were hoping God's promises to their people would be fulfilled. The day the tiny Child came, their waiting was rewarded.

"Now dismiss your servant in peace, O Lord, because my eyes have seen your salvation," Simeon said as he took the child in his arms.

May we see what he saw. Give us eyes of faith, O Lord. Renew our hope, reward our waiting, and fill our hearts with joy.

One Our Father, ten Hail Marys and one Glory Be to the Father.

FIFTH JOYFUL MYSTERY

Finding the Child Jesus in the Temple

"After three days they found Jesus in the Temple, sitting among the teachers and asking them questions."   LUKE 1, 46

Meditation

A special joy comes from finding what we thought lost or seeing what what we were anxious about turn out for the best. The Joyful Mysteries of the Rosary are about such joys: The joys that follow fear, sorrow, struggle and uncertainty.

Look at Mary and Joseph searching for their lost son for three days. Finding Him, their sorrow turns to joy. The lesson is simple: God makes our hearts for joy and will not let us lose treasures that truly matter. Our joy comes from seeking Him.

"Ask and you shall receive, seek and you shall find, knock and it shall be opened to you,"
Jesus teaches.

One Our Father, ten Hail Marys, one Glory Be to the Father and one Hail Holy Queen.

The Five Luminous Mysteries

Thursdays
FIRST LUMINOUS MYSTERY
The Baptism of Christ
Jesus is baptized in the Jordan River by
John the Baptist.

SECOND LUMINOUS MYSTERY
The Wedding at Cana
Jesus attends a wedding at Cana in
Galilee, where he turns water into wine.

THIRD LUMINOUS MYSTERY
**The Proclamation of the Kingdom
of God**
Jesus goes through the towns and cities
of his own country proclaiming God's
Kingdom and helping the poor.

FOURTH LUMINOUS MYSTERY
The Transfiguration
Jesus leads his friends up a high mountain,
where they see him shining in glorious light.

FIFTH LUMINOUS MYSTERY
The Institution of the Holy Eucharist
At supper with his friends before he dies,
Jesus gives himself to them in bread and wine.

The Luminous Mysteries

1st Luminous Mystery
Baptism of Christ

Jesus is baptized in the River Jordan by John the Baptist.

5th Luminous Mystery
Institution of Holy Eucharist

At supper with his friends before he dies, Jesus gives himself to them in bread and wine.

2nd Luminous Mystery
Wedding at Cana

Jesus attends a wedding at Cana in Galilee, where he turns water into wine.

4th Luminous Mystery
Transfiguration

Jesus leads friends up a high mountain, where they see him shining in glorious light.

3rd Luminous Mystery
Proclamation of Kingdom of God

Jesus goes through the towns and cities of his own country proclaiming God's Kingdom and helping the poor.

FIRST LUMINOUS MYSTERY

The Baptism of Jesus

Jesus came from Nazareth in the province of Galilee, and was baptized by John in the Jordan.   MARK 1.9

Meditation

Usually the story of Jesus begins with his birth in Bethlehem, but New Testament sources such as the Gospel of Mark begin his story with his Baptism. After that, Jesus "went about doing good works and healing all who were in the grip of the devil, and God was with him." (Acts 10,38)

From the heavens, God says, "You are my beloved Son; in you I am well pleased. (Mark 1,11) Jesus is God's only Son. But in Baptism his followers become children of God too. With no claim of our own, we are invited by him into God's family and we go in his name to bring goodness and healing to the world in which we live.

By the mystery of your Baptism, Lord, have mercy on us.

One Our Father, ten Hail Marys, one Glory Be to the Father.

SECOND LUMINOUS MYSTERY

The Wedding at Cana

There was a wedding in the town of Cana, in Galilee. Jesus' mother was there, and Jesus and his disciples had also been invited.   JOHN 2,1

Meditation

John's Gospel states that Jesus' public ministry began at a wedding feast that was heading for failure. The wine was running out, which meant the joy of the celebration would be dampened and the couple and their families would be embarrassed.

By changing water into wine, Jesus saved the day. His first miracle brought joy to a group of men and women. In fact, this is why he came: to bring "great joy to all people."

"Do whatever he tells you," his mother Mary said. Following Jesus can bring great joy to us too.

One Our Father, ten Hail Marys, one Glory Be to the Father.

THIRD LUMINOUS MYSTERY

The Proclamation of the Kingdom of God

Jesus went all over Galilee, teaching in the synagogues, preaching the Good News about the Kingdom, and healing people who had all kinds of disease and sickness.

MARK 4, 23

Meditation

After his Baptism in the Jordan, Jesus left the quiet safety of Nazareth to preach the Good News about the Kingdom. Crowds surrounded him as he went through Galilee, and he lifted their hearts with his words.

"I am the light of the world," he said, and he told them to let their light shine before all. "I am the resurrection and the life," he said, and he promised that those who believe in him would live, even though they die. "I am among you as one who serves," he said, and he healed the sick and the troubled. "I am the good shepherd," he said, "and I am willing to die for the sheep." John 10,11

"This, then, is what I command you: love one another." This was his great commandment.

One Our Father, ten Hail Marys and one Glory Be to the Father.

FOURTH LUMINOUS MYSTERY

The Transfiguration

"Jesus took Peter, James, and John with him and went up a mountain to pray. While he was praying, his face changed in appearance, and his clothes became dazzling white." LUKE 9,28-29

Meditation

On the way to Jerusalem where he would be crucified, Jesus told his disciples of his coming sufferings and death. They were deeply saddened. To raise their spirits, Jesus took them up a mountain and he was transfigured before them to show that God's glory endures, even in life's saddest moments.

Even now, God's glory shines in the darkest places of our lives, if we hold them up to the light of faith. Even now, we are given intimations, brief encounters, transfigurations of a lesser kind, as we confront the mystery of suffering.

It is not God's will that the Cross burden us too much. Even now, Jesus reveals his glory to us as we go through life, that we not lose heart.

One Our Father, ten Hail Marys and one Glory Be to the Father.

FIFTH LUMINOUS MYSTERY
The Institution of the Holy Eucharist

"I am the bread of life," Jesus told them. "Those who come to me will never be hungry; those who believe in me will never be thirsty."   JOHN 6, 35

Meditation

On the night before he died, Jesus gave his friends a lasting sign of his love for them. He gave them his body and his blood. For all the ages, he would be their bread of life. Through bread and wine, he gave them his body and blood.

"Those who eat my flesh and drink my blood have eternal life, and I will raise them to life on the last day." Jesus reveals to us that he will lead us to eternal life if we follow him.

One Our Father, ten Hail Marys, one Glory Be to the Father and one Hail Holy Queen.

The Five Sorrowful Mysteries

Tuesdays and Fridays
FIRST SORROWFUL MYSTERY
The Agony in the Garden
Jesus prays in the Garden of Olives
and drops of blood break through
His skin.

SECOND SORROWFUL MYSTERY
The Scourging of Jesus at the Pillar
Jesus is tied to a pillar and cruelly
beaten with whips.

THIRD SORROWFUL MYSTERY
Jesus Is Crowned with Thorns
A crown of thorns is placed upon
Jesus' head.

FOURTH SORROWFUL MYSTERY
Jesus Carries His Cross
Jesus is made to carry His cross
to Calvary.

FIFTH SORROWFUL MYSTERY
The Crucifixion
Jesus is nailed to the cross, and
dies for our sins.

The Sorrowful Mysteries

Tuesdays and Fridays

1st Sorrowful Mystery
Agony in the Garden

At Gethsemane
Jesus prays as
He contemplates the
sins of the World.

5th Sorrowful Mystery
The Crucifixion

Jesus is nailed to
the cross and
dies after three
hours of Agony.

2nd Sorrowful Mystery
The Scourging

Jesus is cruelly
scourged until
His mortified
body could bear
no more.

4th Sorrowful Mystery
Carrying of the Cross

Jesus carries the
heavy cross upon
His shoulders to
Calvary.

3rd Sorrowful Mystery
Crowning with Thorns

A crown of thorns
is placed on the
head of Jesus.

FIRST SORROWFUL MYSTERY

The Agony in the Garden

"They went to a place called Gethsemane... and Jesus became fearful and agitated."   MARK 14, 32

Meditation

Alone on that dark night, among the olive trees in a garden called Gethsemane, Jesus became fearful and disturbed. He could have fled, as His disciples would soon flee. But He stayed, kneeling on the ground, praying to His Father that the cup of suffering pass Him by, yet trusting He could drink it if it be God's will.

As He prayed His spirit grew stronger, and He rose to face what would come.

Help us face, O Lord, the darkness where we are tempted and weak and steady us when we are afraid. By the mystery of your prayer and agony in the garden, have mercy on us!

One Our Father, ten Hail Marys and one Glory Be to the Father.

SECOND SORROWFUL MYSTERY

The Scourging of Jesus at the Pillar

"Pilate, wishing to please the crowd, released Barabbas, and had Jesus scourged." MARK 15, 15

Meditation

Seized in the garden, questioned and falsely accused, Jesus was condemned by Pilate, the Roman governor, to be crucified. He was judged a revolutionary, a danger to the people. And the first step for quick Roman justice was scourging: Jesus was lashed with a punishing whip, His body tracked by painful strokes of blood.

"By His stripes we were healed," the Prophet Isaiah said of You, O Lord.

By the wounds of Your scourging, heal us, O Lord.

One Our Father, ten Hail Marys and one Glory Be to the Father.

Lüberoff

THIRD SORROWFUL MYSTERY

Jesus Is Crowned with Thorns

"The soldiers clothed him in a purple cloak and placing a crown of thorns they put it on Him."   MARK 15, 17

Meditation

The Roman soldiers who were to crucify Jesus called their companions to join them in a cruel act of mockery before they led Him to the place of execution. Jesus had claimed to be king; He spoke of a kingdom. Taking His own clothes from Him, the soldiers draped Him in a ragged purple cloak, the color of royalty, and put on His head a crown of sharp thorns. Then they knelt before Him, struck Him, and spat upon Him, saying, "Hail, King of the Jews!"

O Lord Jesus, made a fool and mocked, uphold the dignity of those demeaned by violence and brutality.

One Our Father, ten Hail Marys and one Glory Be to the Father.

FOURTH SORROWFUL MYSTERY

Jesus Carries His Cross

"And He went out bearing His own cross,
to the place of the skull, called Golgotha."
JOHN 19, 17

Meditation

From the place of judgment, where He
was scourged and mocked, Jesus was led,
carrying His cross, outside Jerusalem's walls
to Golgotha. Hardly able to walk, He
stumbled along the narrow city streets,
hurried by the soldiers who wanted a quick
execution. Many along the way taunted
Him. Most of His friends had deserted Him.
Only a few stayed close by His side. Yet,
though He seemed at the end of His
strength, Jesus kept on.

O Lord Jesus Christ,
you carried your cross.
Be our hope and our strength.

One Our Father, ten Hail Marys and one Glory Be to
the Father.

FIFTH SORROWFUL MYSTERY

The Crucifixion

"And they crucified Him, and divided His clothes among them casting lots to decide what each should take."   MARK 15, 24

Meditation

With dreadful skill, the soldiers nailed Jesus to the cross and set it up against the dark sky. "Father, forgive them for they do not know what they are doing," He prayed. He also promised forgiveness to the thief at his side. And seeing His mother, He said to His disciple with her, "Behold, your mother." Though they might kill Him, the love that filled His life would not die. Even the hardened soldiers recognized greatness in this pitiable man. "Truly, He was God's Son!" the centurion exclaimed.

Lord Jesus Christ, who died for us,
give us a love like Yours.

One Our Father, ten Hail Marys, one Glory Be to the Father and one Hail Holy Queen.

The Five Glorious Mysteries

Wednesdays and Sundays
FIRST GLORIOUS MYSTERY
The Resurrection of Jesus
Jesus rises from the dead, three days
after His death.

SECOND GLORIOUS MYSTERY
The Ascension of Jesus
Forty days after His death, Jesus
ascends into heaven.

THIRD GLORIOUS MYSTERY
The Descent of the Holy Spirit
Ten days after the Ascension, the Holy
Spirit comes to the apostles and the
Blessed Mother in the form of fiery tongues.

FOURTH GLORIOUS MYSTERY
The Assumption of Mary in Heaven
The Blessed Virgin dies and is
assumed into heaven.

FIFTH GLORIOUS MYSTERY
The Crowning of Mary
The Blessed Virgin is crowned Queen
of Heaven and Earth by Jesus, her Son.

The Glorious Mysteries

Wednesdays and Sundays

1st Glorious Mystery
The Resurrection

Jesus rises glorious
and immortal,
three days after
His death.

5th Glorious Mystery
The Coronation

Mary is
gloriously crowned
Queen of Heaven
and Earth.

2nd Glorious Mystery
The Ascension

Jesus ascends into
Heaven forty days
after His
Resurrection.

4th Glorious Mystery
The Assumption

The Blessed
Mother is united
with her Divine
Son in heaven.

3rd Glorious Mystery
**Descent of the
Holy Spirit**

The Holy Spirit
descends upon
Mary and the
Apostles.

FIRST GLORIOUS MYSTERY

The Resurrection of Jesus

The angel said: "Do not be afraid...He is not here, He is risen as He said."

MATTHEW 28, 5-6

Meditation

On Easter Sunday, the women coming to anoint the body of Jesus were sent away from the tomb, the place of death. "He is not here," the angel said, "He is risen."

Then Jesus appeared to His disciples, sometimes to one and other times to many. Soon even the most doubtful, like Thomas, were convinced. No, it was not a ghost or their imagination. They could touch His wounds with their hands. Jesus was risen from the dead.

O Lord Jesus Christ, conqueror of death,
help us who believe in You to rise again.

One Our Father, ten Hail Marys and one Glory Be to the Father.

SECOND GLORIOUS MYSTERY

The Ascension of Jesus

"As the apostles looked on, Jesus was taken up into heaven out of their sight."

ACTS 1, 9

Meditation

After appearing to His disciples for over forty days, Jesus disappeared from their sight. The gospels see the risen Jesus having a further mission than just returning to life. He has a mission to begin a new creation.

"I go to prepare a place for you," Jesus promises His disciples at the Last Supper. Ascending into heaven, that is what He does: He prepares a place for us, new heavens and a new earth. A home that is ours because of His love for us. It is not only the world of here and now we hope for; we have a home above.

"O Jesus Christ, returned to heaven in victory, remember my flesh in which you were born."

ST. HILARY

One Our Father, ten Hail Marys and one Glory Be to the Father.

THIRD GLORIOUS MYSTERY

The Descent of the Holy Spirit

"They were filled with the Holy Spirit and began to speak in tongues as they were given power to speak."   ACTS 2, 2

Meditation

"I will not leave you orphans," Jesus told His disciples. They were to wait for the promised gift of the Father– the gift of the Holy Spirit.

So they waited in Jerusalem until the Jewish feast of Pentecost, fifty days after Easter. Then, as they were all together in one place, a strong wind and sound filled the house, and flames like tongues of fire came to rest on them. They were filled with the Holy Spirit.

The Holy Spirit is Jesus' "first gift to those who believe, to complete His work on earth and bring us the fullness of grace."

"Come, Holy Spirit, Creator come from Your bright heav'nly throne: come take possession of our souls, and make them all Your own."

One Our Father, ten Hail Marys and one Glory Be to the Father.

FOURTH GLORIOUS MYSTERY

The Assumption of Mary in Heaven

"We believe that Jesus died and rose again. Through Jesus, God will bring to life those who have fallen asleep."

1 THESSALONIANS 4, 14

Meditation

A long tradition supports our belief that Mary, the mother of Jesus, was assumed body and soul into heaven. God rewarded her for faithfully fulfilling her role as the Mother of Jesus. And so, she was brought to life after falling asleep in death. She was taken up into heaven.

We see her as a sign of what our future holds. In the words of the church's liturgy, she brings "hope and comfort for your people on their pilgrim way."

Pray for us, O holy Mother of God,
that we may be made worthy
of the promises of Christ.

One Our Father, ten Hail Marys and one Glory Be to the Father.

FIFTH GLORIOUS MYSTERY

The Crowning of Mary

"A great sign appeared in the heavens, a woman clothed with the sun, the moon under her feet, and on her head a crown of twelve stars."   REV 12, 1

Meditation

The mysteries of the Rosary begin with a sign the Prophet Isaiah gave: "This is a sign to you: a virgin shall conceive and bear a son, and you will call His name Emmanuel, 'God with us.'" They end urging us to look heavenward, to the sign of a woman clothed in the glories of God's kingdom. Mary, because she stood loyally beside her Son, has become a powerful intercessor at the side of Christ, our heavenly king. She will be a mother to us.

Hail Holy Queen,
mother of mercy,
our life, our sweetness and our hope.
To you we cry,
poor banished children of Eve.

One Our Father, ten Hail Marys, one Glory Be to the Father and one Hail Holy Queen.

Litany of the Blessed Virgin Mary

Lord, have mercy,

Christ, have mercy,

Lord, have mercy.

Christ, hear us.

Christ, graciously hear us.

God, the Father of heaven, have mercy on us.

God, the Son, Redeemer of the world, have mercy on us.

God, the Holy Spirit, have mercy on us.

Holy Trinity, one God, have mercy on us.

Holy Mary,

(after each invocation, respond with, "Pray for us")

-Pray for us.

Holy Mother of God,

Holy Virgin of virgins,

Mother of Christ,

Mother, full of grace,

Mother most pure,

Mother most chaste,
Immaculate Mother,
Sinless Mother,
Lovable Mother,
Model of mothers,
Mother of good counsel,
Mother of our Maker,
Mother of our Savior,
Wisest of virgins,
Holiest of virgins,
Virgin, powerful in the sight of God,
Virgin, merciful to us sinners,
Virgin, faithful to all God asks of you,
Mirror of holiness,
Seat of wisdom,
Cause of our joy,
Shrine of the Spirit,
Honor of your people,
Devoted handmaid of the Lord,
Tower of David,
Tower of ivory,
House of gold,

Ark of the covenant,

Gate of heaven,

Star of hope,

Health of the sick,

Refuge of sinners,

Comfort of the afflicted,

Help of Christians,

Queen of angels,

Queen of patriarchs,

Queen of prophets,

Queen of apostles,

Queen of martyrs,

Queen of confessors,

Queen of virgins,

Queen of all saints,

Queen conceived in holiness,

Queen raised up to glory,

Queen of the Rosary,

Queen of peace,

Lamb of God, you take away the sins
    of the world, – Spare us, O Lord.

Lamb of God, you take away the sins

of the world,

    – Graciously hear us, O Lord.

Lamb of God, you take away the sins
    of the world,

    – Have mercy on us.

Pray for us, O holy Mother of God,

    – That we may be made worthy
      of the promises of Christ.

Let us pray.

Lord God,

  give to your people the joy of
  continual health in mind and body.

With the prayers of the Virgin Mary
  to help us, guide us through
  the sorrows of this life to
  eternal happiness in the life to come

We ask this through Christ our Lord.

  Amen.

6.
Meditate on 3rd Mystery, saying the "Our Father," ten "Hail Marys" and the "Glory Be."

7.
Meditate on 4th Mystery, saying the "Our Father," ten "Hail Marys" and the "Glory Be."

5.
Meditate on 2nd Mystery, saying the "Our Father," ten "Hail Marys" and the "Glory Be."

8.
Meditate on 5th Mystery, saying the "Our Father," ten "Hail Marys" and the "Glory Be."

4.
Meditate on 1st Mystery, saying the "Our Father," ten "Hail Marys" and the "Glory Be."

9.
Concluding prayer, "Hail Holy Queen"

3.
Say three "Hail Marys" and the "Glory Be."

2.
Say the "Our Father".

1.
Make the Sign of the Cross, say the Apostles' Creed.